Pilgrims

Books by Jean Valentine

Dream Barker *and Other Poems*

Pilgrims

Jean Valentine : Pilgrims

FARRAR, STRAUS AND GIROUX, NEW YORK

Library of Congress catalog card number:
70-93514
Printed in the United States of America
Published simultaneously in Canada by
Doubleday Canada Ltd., Toronto
First printing, 1969
Designed by Cynthia Krupat

Grateful acknowledgment is made to the
following, who first printed some of these poems:
Poetry for "The Summer House," "Orpheus and
Eurydice," "Separation," "Dearest," "April,"
"Broken-down Girl," "Archangel," and
"Photograph of Delmore Schwartz"; *Yale Review*
for "The Couples," "By the Boat Pond," and
"Thinking About Cain"; *American Scholar* for
"Fireside" (originally "Our Saragasso");
Commonweal for "Solomon"; *Radcliffe Quarterly*
for "In the Museum"; *The New Yorker* for
"The Torn-down Building"; *Colloquy* for
"Moon Man" and "Visiting Day at School"
(read as the Phi Beta Kappa poem at Swarthmore
College in June, 1968); and to Random House,
publisher of Olga Carlisle's *Poets on Street
Corners*, in whose pages the Ahkmadulina
adaptation, "Goodbye," originally appeared.

With gratitude

to Mr. Gerald Freund,

and The Rockefeller Foundation;

and to Miss Constance Smith,

and The Radcliffe Institute

Poems

I

II

II

ἔγω δὲ κῆν᾽ ὅττω
τις ἔραται

"... but I say whatever
one loves, is "

SAPPHO

I

The Couples

One night they all
found themselves alone,
their first force gone.
No law.

Vacations were no vacation,
nothing came in the mail,
and so on. Everyone
wanted to be good,

no one alive remembered them.

Out of decency no one spoke.
By the time day broke
even the babies were bored with them,
with hunger, and falling;

even you, Prince, gray
around the mouth and tired of calling,
tired of briars, tired of them,
had ridden away.

Fireside

The fox went under the garden
thinking. The watersnake
never moved, or the sun.
—Night, and everyone's straight out

longing; the cat's in the woods,
the children lie loose in stories
tall as this world could
be if we could run for it Lord

Fox. Foxfire will, we thought, out,
you and I, blue glass at the fireside side by side,
word for word,
wood for wood,
desire for desire,
nicer than God.

Solomon

Still, gold, open-handed,
sad King Solomon
listened: they started,
weightless, close to his ear,
sweet as bees.

One with light breasts and knees
danced with herself before Solomon,
one stood by with barbarian eyes
mad for Solomon,
one, a child, even touched his face

and he smiled in his clothes,
shut his eyes.

Solomon sat by a white pond
his skin thin gold
and his head down.

One stood by with barbarian eyes
mad for Solomon.
She came to his hands,

light, far, anyone
or no one. Solomon
touched her eyes.

                        Too close,
too heavy, the dark
did just what it had promised,

the park turned sharp as it had started:

he closed his hands.

In the Museum

There is a stone
where the Buddha was.
Nothing: air,

one footprint; his chair
a stone.
We stood

back, out of harm;
smiled; right?
went on.

The next room, love,
was funnier: all that love-making
in broad daylight,

and every one of them smiling.
Back where the Buddha was, the stone,
happy as God,

grinned like bone,
love: the air,
asking nothing,

smiled everywhere.

Come.

By the Boat Pond

FOR S

The newspapers blowing over the street
made her cry, all the birds in New York were crying
because they couldn't speak Greek,

she took nothing with her and went out onto the street.
The day was obscure, one more
lick of the quiet
licking at the door,

her soft black magic,
swallowing him, the children,
the world: leaving, everyone leaving,
all turning angels or nothing,

nothing or swimming like paradise children.

The Summer House

i

She took his hand
so he brought her to his country:
'See it is dry': and

it was a light field, water,
a tree loud as water
in that wind.

—In your country
there is a light field, water.

Your body is in this wind,
I am in your mouth, your hand.

ii

There were times
out of time's drag
we'd be without fixed faces
bodies or words; times

held like a feathery scene
on a Quimper plate: v's of quick birds
in their aviary sky, blue flowers
strung all around the dot-faced boy and girl:

all afternoon the sunlight ticked across
sleep, across our borrowed house.

iii

The angels we made in the snow
are blown and the shapes at the snow's edge
are only themselves again

and we our taller selves
smoke between the house and the woods' edge,
dying to come in or have snow:

—Does he love her? She loves,
he loves, they

love the old stories of the snow
and the look of the house. Together so.

Woods

Dearest darling woodenhead
I love you

I can taste you
in bed laughing

come on Teach I love your
hair

Penseroso,
crab, you angel!

feel me on the palm of your hand?

Look

all the thin trees
are hanging this morning ready to fuzz,

high birds I can't see are whistling,
winter's dripping down

faster and faster and
faster. And not to death.

Wait.

Her dream: the child

FOR M.R

It stared and stared
right through them to the world.

But it better come in said
a quiet man and she said Look
and took it into bed.

They lay closer
in the pale morning. Three flat white ducks
on the wall woke up and took off.

In the morning
he woke them up humming.

Orpheus and Eurydice

'What we spent, we had.
What we had, we have.
What we lost, we leave.'

—Epitaph for his wife and himself,
by the Duke of Devon, 12th century

i

You. You running across the field.

A hissing second, not a word,
and there it was, our underworld:
behind your face another, and another,
and I

away.

—And you alive: staring,
almost smiling;

hearing them come down, tearing
air from air.

ii

'This dark is everywhere'
we said, and called it light,
coming to ourselves.
                    Fear
has at me, dearest. Even this night
drags down. The moon's gone. Someone
shakes an old black camera-cloth
in front of our eyes.
Yours glint like a snowman's eyes.
We just look on, at each other.

What we had, we have. They circle down.
You draw them down like flies.
You laugh, we run
over a red field, turning at the end to blue air,—
you turning, turning again! the river
tossing a shoe up, a handful of hair.

Goodbye

AFTER BELLA AHKMADULINA

And finally I'll say goodbye.
Don't feel you have to love.
I'm chattering, crazy,
or maybe coming into a crazier kind of peace.

How you loved! Your lips just grazing over disaster,
tasting nothing. But that doesn't matter.
How you loved! How you destroyed!
Offhandedly, like a great pale curious boy.

O coldness of failure, cold certainty,
there's no settling with you. The body
wanders around, sees light; sun and moon
shine through the glass pane.

The empty body goes on with its little task.
But the hands fall light and slack,
and like a small flock, sideways,
all sounds and smells graze off away.

Separation

i

OK my child
but not unmake
the smudge of black
under his eyes, their eyes,

or turn it back to the quiet, best
time we sat
in the front room; dumb,
dressed, affectionate.

ii

There is fear there, but you know
it's fear. Why,
summer's just going to be starting;
I have work,
I have friends,
I have whatever I had.

I mean to take hold
like a tree. There's tar,
bolts, wires. Leaves.

The trees rattle all around.
Jack and Elizabeth live in a hidden house
and hold hands in it;

they smile at me as if in the past,
as if kindly. O Jack and Elizabeth will you marry
marry you will Elizabeth and Jack o. Jack is

rubbing her back
down in front of the summer fire
her eyes are apple green.

Out of the blue, your face
bent over some book you love.

To bed. Sheet lightning on sheet glass, a morning
enough. Enough
I don't understand:

these wires. The white
wet root here
now. These people's bread.

iii

The children make spy-maps of the neighbors for you
and paste leaves on. The river wind blows the leaves,
the neighbors rock on cinders hour to hour,
hot. I watch nights from my sliding corner
out to where you are: the street, where your
back goes walking, talking,
talking. You take daylight,
and the law, the way things tick.
And us, wherever you go, —leaves,
how we float, and stick!

iv

Breaking. I just sit. Well,
I hear noises.

I hope to hear noises, wishes
lip up over the steps all night:

flying fish,
my own breathing.

Without knowing anything,
without money, America,
without leaving,

coming to a new country.
Your two hands,
a few names.

Over and over without a smile
the little walls break up and bleed
pure violence and mend and mend.

Thinking about Cain

FOR H.C

> God to Cain: 'and if thou doest not well,
> sin lieth at the door. And unto thee shall be
> his desire, and thou shalt rule over him.'

The first life's blood. Now day
lies at the door, the clocks tick,
the smoky kitten nurses at my salty fingers,
not the best. Six-thirty, time

to get up, to get the children up,
to find the mother,
the father.
In the holes they left. Doors!

Ways open to befriend our friends,
our words, our worst old ways, to learn

to love this circling through and through
the veins of those two that day, *thou.*

Dearest,

             this day broke
at ten degrees. I swim
in bed over some dream sentence lost
at a child's crying: the giant on her wall
tips the room over, back:
I tell her all I know,
the walls will settle, he'll go.

Holding her fingers, I watch the sky rise, white.
The frost makes about the same lines
on the same window as last winter,
quicker, quieter. . I think how nothing's happened,

how to know
to touch a face to make a line
to break the ice to come in time
into this world, unlikely, small,
bloody, shiny, is all, is God's good will
I think, I turn to you,
and fail, and turn,

as the day widens
and we don't know what to do.

II

April

Suppose we are standing together a minute
on the wire floor of a *gaswagen:*
suppose we are in the dark.

It's warm and dry.
We have food.
We aren't in hiding waiting, mostly
we're sitting in our own light rooms.

Come over, bring things: bring
milk, peanut butter,
your pills, your woollens, crayons.

Nuns pray.
Snow. It's dark.
Pray for our friends who died
last year and the year
before and who will die this year.

Let's speak,
as the bees do.

Broken-down Girl

Imagine her quick
who could talk
and cry, still
running, under
the whole sky,
the youngest sister,

who fumbled down
in such sincere pieces.
Silver pieces!
The wind,
the Virginia rain,
touch your face

now none of us
at this table
could, frail
gleam, glass face
without a back,
open book,
telstar.

Bin Dream, West Cottage East, D-11

You or I,

sweet Mag, miserable sixteen, paternal,
put the kettle on,
set out three white cups,
and forgot,

the minister edged up sideways
with a certain amount of floor to cross
to the silver sink the radio
the fireplace and the cup,

the sky inched into blue-white milk,
the housemother stood up,
looking at us all, not warmly,
said, *No one*

ate, Mag
put the kettle on

you, your father, your married sister,
or I

Bin Dream #2, Interview with Stravinsky

"Gossip is travel,
and in these times, like travel,
speeded up to the nth degree,
and that's alright,

if you remember of an afternoon
the immeasurable sift
of geological time, the slowness
of say slow snow,

                    gossip deriving
from the ancient aramaic
word, *sari*, or *safari*,

meaning
to travel,
or, *to love*."

Death House

It was the same kind of night, the light, the coughing,
huge shoes walking, your breathing
through three walls, sleeping into the last things.
In the corner of our grove
the newest one kept on saying
oh, I, oh, I,
Oh him, the guard grinned, going by,
and woke you up. You went ahead.

The guard went ahead.
This is the room, here come the City's dead,
grave sisters, fur-trapping fathers,
mothers still waiting, falling
past my free hands,
and my hands falling.

Archangel

It's dark in here,
your halo looks flat as a plate.
Maybe we're still there. Was that lightning?

You look like a cat when you sleep.
I'm not sleeping. You reading?
I'm looking for this poem,

about a cat—wait a minute—
Go on.
You can read to me all you want.

That time it was lightning.
Is it you? Rolling the green grass back?
I love it when you smile like that.

Is this the white dawn, Angel, in the book?
It's dawn. Look.
Where are they bringing the rock back?

Where are you going?

Half an Hour

Hurt, hurtful, snake-charmed,
struck white together half an hour we tear
through the half-dark after

some sweet core,
under, over gravity,
some white shore. .

spin, hidden one, *spin*,
trusted to me! laugh sore tooth
sucked warm, sweet; sweet wine

running cool through new
dry shrewd turnings of my soul,
opening veins.

Gull-feathers beating,
beating! Gliding. Still,
sidelong eye. . wings beating

like words against my eyes.
And your eyes—
o brother-animal, mild,

terrible! —your eyes wait, have been waiting,
knowing,
unknowable, on that sky shore.

A life is waiting.
Its webbed hand
reached out. .

Trust me!
truth-
telling fish of the sky!

your hand beyond my hand,
your phosphorous trail
broken, lost.

Visiting Day at School

'She knows she can rub some of her
brown skin off and use it for coloring.'
—A mother, to Robert Coles

The tall, good, raw-boned, wrong
teacher teaches wrong
glory the children shuffle back from dumb

as we do, too,
having got the problem
right:

what you hold
in your hand
is your hand:

You shall all have prizes, and the last,
they say, first: to come home free,
warm and bare, to laugh to see, Jack,

see the years run
around the tree
to melt to feed you,

Jane, see the line the days flew,
quick bird, down around the thumb,
almost straight,

through all the king's gold,
back.

The Child Jung

'What will become of the boy?'
—his father

"This stone is,
was for ages,
and will be: knows I know,

and it's good, hidden,
hidden I'm a great old doctor, whirling,

an eighteenth-century man whirling
through the woods in a light green carriage,

buckles on my shoes. . Schoolboy!
the filthiest boy ever made,

or blessed. . oh curled black
shivering freak!
O my stone God quicksand Eternity!"

Coltrane, Syeeda's Song Flute

'When I came across it on the piano it reminded
me of her, because it sounded like a happy,
child's song.' —Coltrane

FOR M & P.R

To Marilyn, to Peter,
playing, making things: the walls, the stairs,
the attics, bright nests in nests;
the slow, light, grave unstitching of lies,
opening, stinking, letting in air

you bear yourselves in, become your own mother and father,
your own child.
You lying closer.

You going along. Days.
The strobe-lit wheel stops dead
once, twice in a life: old-fashioned rays:

and then all the rest of the time pulls blur,
only you remember it more, playing.

Listening here in the late quiet you can think
great things of us all, I think we will all, Coltrane,
meet speechless and easy in Heaven, our names
known and forgotten, all dearest, all come giant-stepping
out into some wide, light, merciful mind. .

John
Coltrane, 40, gone
right through the floorboards,
up to the shins, up to the eyes,
closed over,

Syeeda's happy, child's song
left up here, playing.

Photograph of Delmore Schwartz

FOR E.L

A young king,
oak, painted and gilded, writing

no one should be so unhappy,
holding his hands out,

but his arms are missing from the shoulders down,
his right side's gone, his mouth's

flaking like a mirror, still
photograph of your childhood,

your son. No one
should be so unhappy, should lie

still in that bending room
where all the atoms fly

off their hooks, animals and children
and friends kill, it was a delusion,

we were not living, the hotel floor
wasn't coming and going and coming

at that great head hurled radiant, flat
at the new world.

The Torn-down Building

Slowly, slowly our exploding time
gives off its lives: a lens, an eyelash rub
under the new ground broken,
under the new primary-colored paint
put up for someone to come to
to start off from to cherish

but dear one this December
the walls walk off, we sit mother-naked
smiling on our boxes of books:
slowly the first snowfall
curls around its own faint fall
each dot different we thought we could
turn back and back to learn, with all this
light everywhere.

The snow falls around as we walk talking war,
books, the times, our friends' funny business.
Lens, eyelash whisper against the flat
stairs outlined in old paint on the open air:
the light draws a thousand thousand window sills,
bottles, our shadows on the floor,
all backs, our piles of books, our toys,
our boxes of letters. Slowly over the newspaper
this quarter century takes in
its infant deaths, gives off its smiling kouroi
and we will meet their eyes in the air

        The January light's stock still
a second from your face to mine, mine to the child's,
her words a flare, a fountain lighter than air.

Moon Man

'Here too we dare to hope.'
—*Romano Guardini*

FOR A.R

Swimming down to us
light years
not always a straight line
that was his joke, his night
fears, his pilgrim's climb.

About half way
throwing his silver
suit away he
sees the green earth
click for the first time:

the lightest girl
the heaviest ocean
coming to themselves
and to his hand.

He sets a comradely couple walking
down his white road,
hospitable; hears a shiny
boy and girl, bird and bird
having a time

in his green water.
Clean against it all
one last hour
all alone the moon man's
open everywhere:

This mass is his salt
his girl
        his sky
his work
        his floor.

The Child and the Terrorist,
The Terrorist and the Child

FOR J.M.C

The globe's on fire in his hands
and everyone's asleep.

What will we feed him when he comes?
Just getting to know his step, his voice,

my step, a way back in the dark
to where I go without telling lies

or leaving anyone, will take a lifetime,
and it's going slowly,

                 and there's that blue-
white shell I turned my back on at my back,

cracked, stuck to me bone by bone,
turning to stone, wanting to drop,
wanting to turn in a cool globe,
wanting to call

—You, how is it with you?
Archaically cut off. Antarctic miles.

Night.

From this night on God let me eat
like that blind child on the train
touching her yogurt as I'd touch a spiderweb
the first morning in the country—sky red—

holding the carton and spoon to her mouth
with all her eyeless body, and then
orientally resting, the whole time smiling
a little to one side of straight ahead.

45

Pilgrims

FOR S & R.F

Standing there they began to grow skins
dappled as trees, alone in the flare
of their own selves: the fire
died down in the open ground

and they made a place for themselves.
It wasn't much good,
they'd fall, and freeze,

some of them said
Well, it was all they could,

some said it was beautiful, some days,
the way the little ones took to the water,
and some lay smoking, smoking,

and some burned up for good,
and some waited,
lasting, staring
over each other's merciful shoulders,
listening:
         only high in a sudden January thaw
or safe a second in some unsmiling eyes
they'd known always

whispering
Why are we in this life.

46